BOXER BOOKS Ltd. and the distinctive Boxer Books logo
are trademarks of Union Square & Co., LLC.
Union Square & Co., LLC, is a subsidiary of Sterling Publishing Co., Inc.

Text © 2024 Boxer Books
Illustrations © 2024 Lo Cole

All rights reserved. No part of this publication may be reproduced,
stored in a retrieval system, or transmitted in any form or by any
means (including electronic, mechanical, photocopying, recording,
or otherwise) without prior written permission from the publisher.

First published in Great Britain in 2024.

ISBN 978-1-4547-1173-5

A catalogue record for this book is available from the British Library.

For information about custom editions, special sales, and premium purchases,
please contact specialsales@unionsquareandco.com.

Printed in China
10 9 8 7 6 5 4 3 2 1

01/24

unionsquareandco.com

Spring Street™ Series created by David Bennett
Written by Sasha Morton
Illustrated by Lo Cole
Series editors: Sasha Morton and Leilani Sparrow
Series consultant: Mary Anne Wolpert, Cambridge University

VEHICLES
Contents

Cars, cars, cars 6

Powerful wheels 8

Bikes and motorcycles 10

Everybody in! 12

Clean wheels 14

Working wheels 16

Get moving! 18

Emergency and military vehicles 20

Working boats 22

Setting sail! 24

Row, row, row your boat! 26

Inland waterways 28

Air and water power 30

Super submersibles 32

In the air! 34

Wheels up! 36

Rail power 38

Long and short rail journeys 40

Connected to cables 42

Lift off! 44

Spring Street

Cars, cars, cars

1 Sedans have a separate boot space behind the passenger seat.

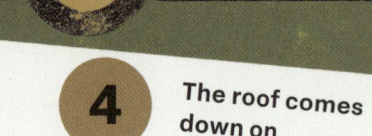

4 The roof comes down on convertibles.

2 A coupe has two doors and a sloping roof.

5 Only the driver and one passenger can fit in a micro car.

3 Sports cars are designed to be driven or raced at high speeds.

The first automobiles were sold over 130 years ago. Over time, cars have changed a lot, but they still have four wheels! **Which of these cars would you like to drive?**

6 SUV stands for Sports Utility Vehicle.

7 Compact SUVs are built for five people.

8 The rear door in a hatchback car swings up instead of out. Don't bump your head!

1 sedan	**3** sports car	**5** micro car	**7** compact SUV
2 coupe	**4** convertible	**6** SUV	**8** hatchback

Powerful wheels

1 Monster trucks have huge wheels.

5 Four-wheel-drive vehicles are built to drive on any road surface.

These wheeled vehicles are fast and strong. Some of them are also very expensive and need special skills to drive! You might be high off the ground or low to the floor, but there is a car for every kind of road.

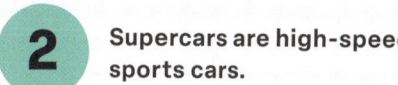

2 Supercars are high-speed sports cars.

The Bugatti Chiron is one of the most powerful cars in the world.

3

4

Formula 1 racing cars can travel at up to 220 miles per hour (350kph)!

1 monster truck

2 supercar

3 Bugatti Chiron

4 Formula 1 racing car

5 Four-wheel-drive vehicle

Bikes and motorcycles

1 The top speed for a motor scooter is 30 miles per hour (48kph).

2 A quad bike has four wheels.

3 Fixed gear racing bikes don't have brakes!

4 BMX bikes are built to be ridden off-road or used as stunt bikes.

Whether you're pedalling a bike for fun or taking part in a race, there's a bike for everyone – just don't forget to wear your helmet!

5 Motocross bikes are good on rough ground, and are fast and loud.

6 Cruiser motorcycles are built to be comfortable to ride.

7 Tandem bicycles are for two people.

1. motor scooter
2. quad bike
3. fixed gear racing bike
4. BMX bike
5. motocross bike
6. cruiser motorcycle
7. tandem bicycle

Everybody in!

1. In many parts of the world, comfortable buses that take people on long journeys are called coaches.

2. Limousines can sometimes carry up to 20 people (or just 1) in luxury.

3. A small bus is called a minibus and can seat up to 16 people.

4.

These vehicles are built for groups. Let's all wave to the yellow school bus and see who's stepping out of the sleek limousine!

5 Double-decker buses were first used in London, England.

Yellow school buses are famous throughout America and painted in National School Bus Glossy Yellow.

6 A Sports Utility Vehicle (SUV) can carry seven or eight people.

- **1** coach
- **2** limousine
- **3** minibus
- **4** school bus
- **5** double-decker bus
- **6** SUV

Clean wheels

1 A tuk-tuk is a three-wheeled electric taxi used in cities.

2 Electric cars need to be plugged in to charge the battery.

3 Formula E cars are raced through city streets on special days.

4 The word *rickshaw* means "human-powered vehicle" in Japanese.

5 Golf carts were invented to take golfers and their equipment around golf courses.

All of these forms of transport use electricity, rechargeable batteries or a person pedalling or pushing them to move. They're a cleaner alternative to vehicles powered by fossil fuels such as petrol or diesel, which are harmful to our planet.

6 To steer a Segway, you just need to lean in the direction you want to go.

7 Electric bicycles take between three to six hours to charge.

8 The first motorised scooters were made in 1915.

9 More than half of all skateboarders in the US live in the state of California.

10 Traditional scooters are usually pushed along with one foot.

1 tuk-tuk
2 electric car
3 Formula E racing car
4 rickshaw
5 golf cart
6 Segway
7 electric bicycle
8 electric scooter
9 skateboard
10 scooter

Working wheels

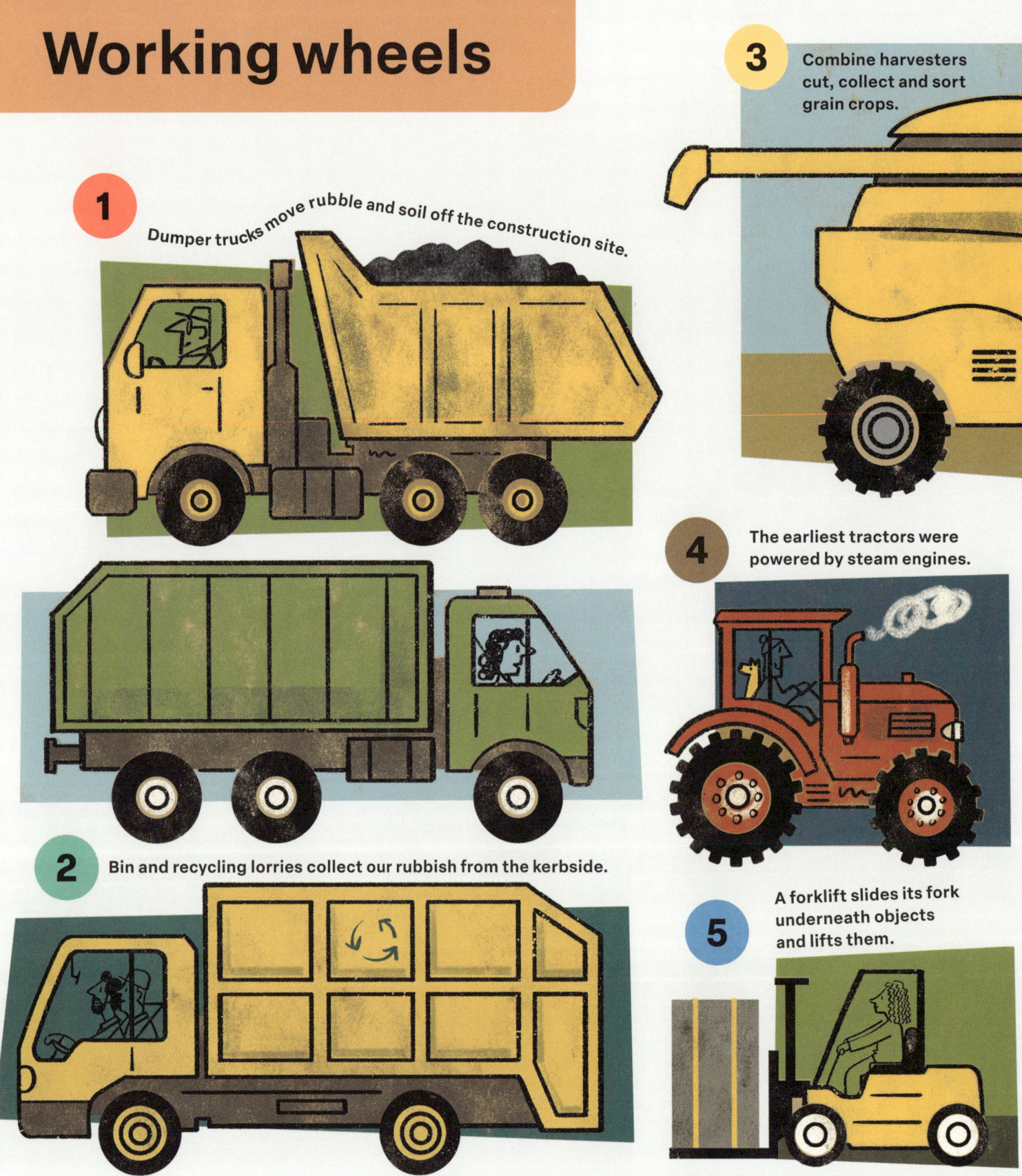

1. Dumper trucks move rubble and soil off the construction site.
2. Bin and recycling lorries collect our rubbish from the kerbside.
3. Combine harvesters cut, collect and sort grain crops.
4. The earliest tractors were powered by steam engines.
5. A forklift slides its fork underneath objects and lifts them.

These hard-working wheels are built to tackle big, tough jobs! You'll often find them on a construction site or farm. **Do you have a favourite construction vehicle?**

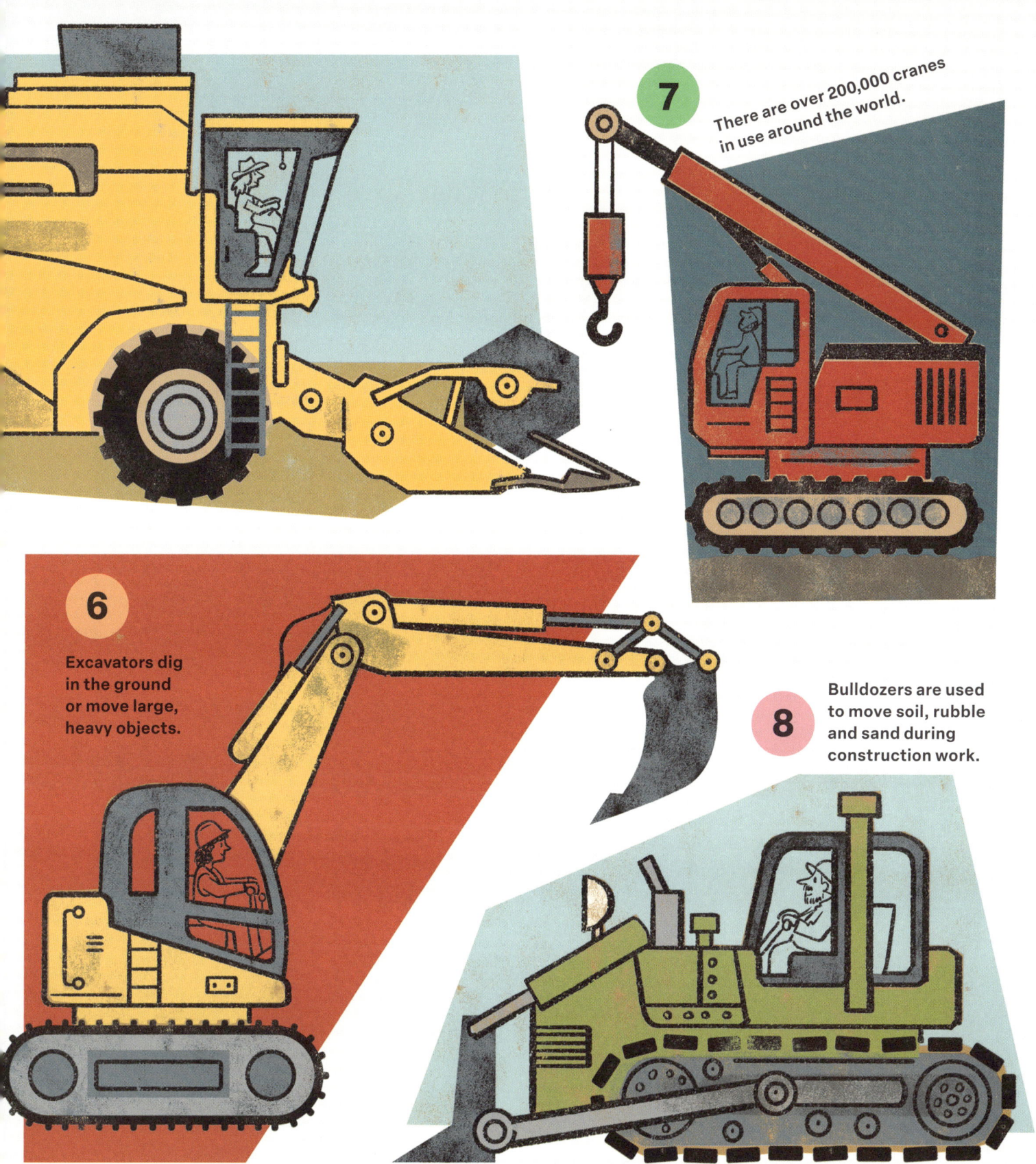

7 There are over 200,000 cranes in use around the world.

6 Excavators dig in the ground or move large, heavy objects.

8 Bulldozers are used to move soil, rubble and sand during construction work.

| 1 | dumper truck | 3 | combine harvester | 5 | forklift | 7 | crane |
| 2 | Bin and recycling lorries | 4 | tractor | 6 | excavator | 8 | bulldozer |

17

Get moving!

1 All-Terrain Vehicles (ATVs) can pull trailers and drive across different types of land.

3 Wide or heavy loads can be moved on an HGV lorry.

5 Transporters can move lots of vehicles at the same time.

The longest truck in the world is based in India and has 148 wheels when its trailer is attached! These vehicles don't have as many wheels as that, but they are still very useful at moving things from one place to another.

2 Tankers can carry fuel or milk.

Delivery vans bring things we have bought to our front door.

Removal lorries take people's belongings from one place to another.

1 ATV and trailer

2 tanker

3 HGV lorry

4 delivery van

5 transporter

6 removal lorry

Emergency and military vehicles

1 The first fire engines were buckets of water on wheels.

2 Route clearance vehicles can dig or move objects off the road using a special claw.

Specially trained teams and crews operate these vehicles. Some of them have loud sirens and flashing lights – these warn people to move out of the way when they are travelling to emergencies.

3 Air ambulances are used when there is no access by road.

4 Police escorts use motorcycles to protect important people travelling in official vehicles, such as world leaders or royalty.

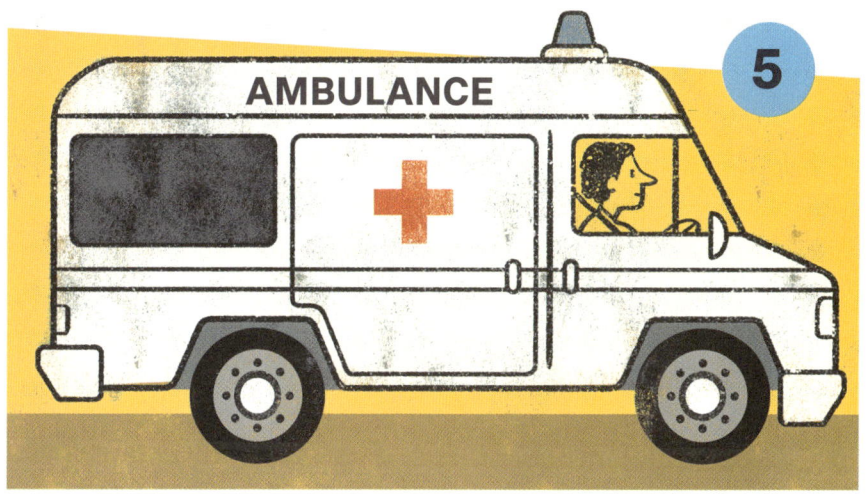

5 The NHS (or National Health Service) ambulance service started in 1948.

6 Amphibious vehicles can be used on land or water.

1 fire engine **3** air ambulance **5** ambulance

2 route clearance vehicle **4** police escort **6** amphibious vehicle

Working boats

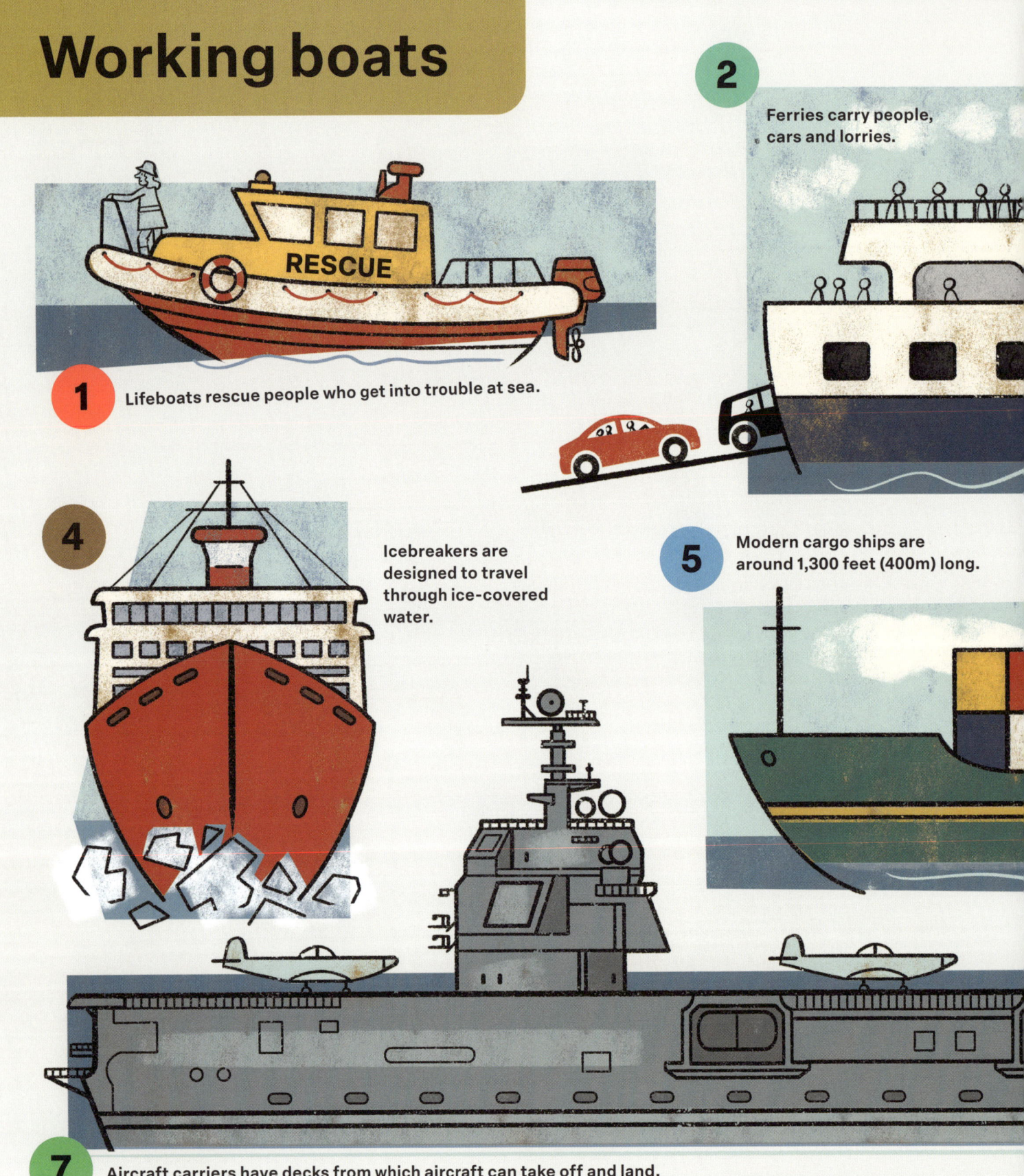

1 Lifeboats rescue people who get into trouble at sea.

2 Ferries carry people, cars and lorries.

4 Icebreakers are designed to travel through ice-covered water.

5 Modern cargo ships are around 1,300 feet (400m) long.

7 Aircraft carriers have decks from which aircraft can take off and land.

Working on a boat is hard work – and definitely not the job for you if you get seasick. Have you ever seen any of these out at sea?

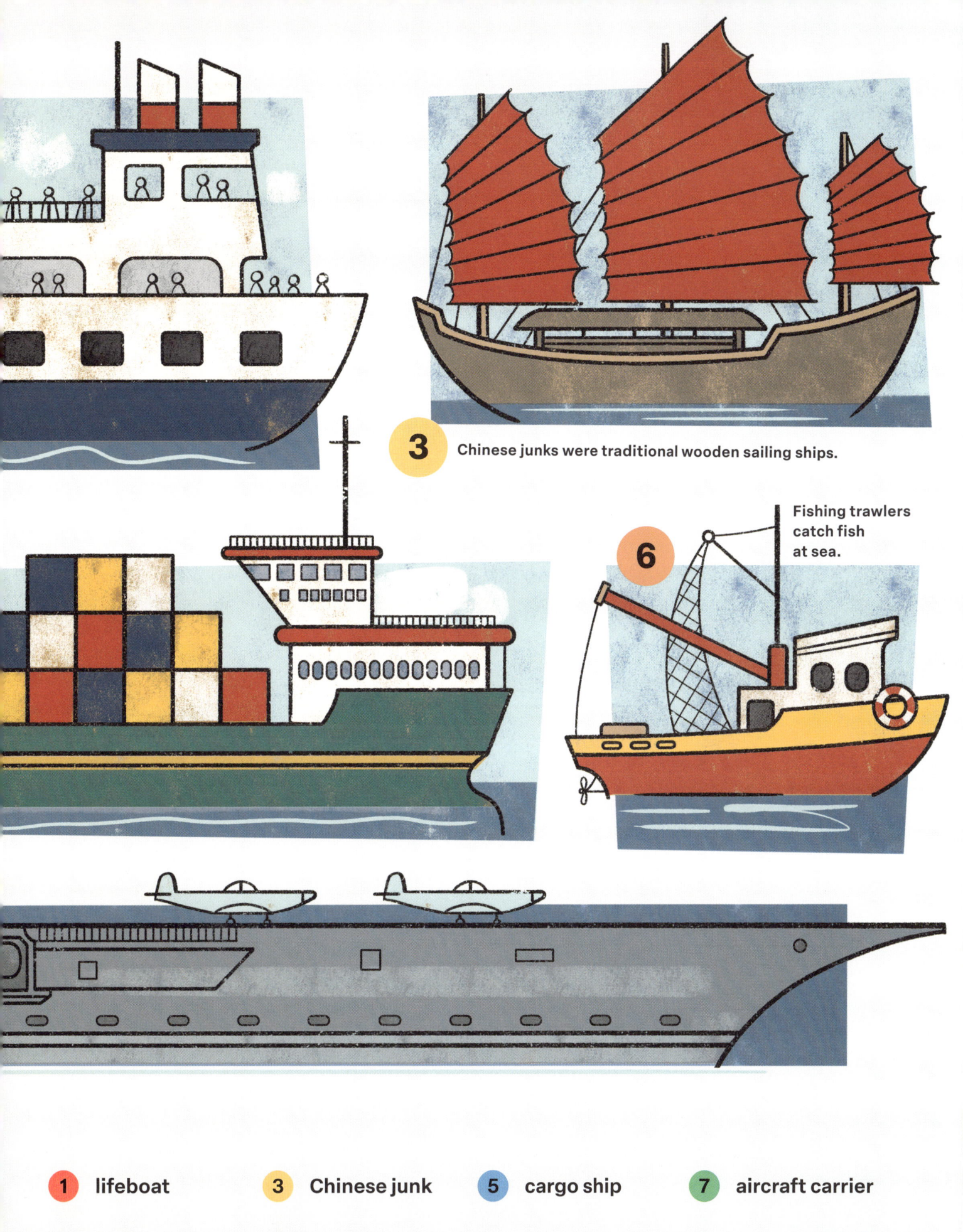

3 Chinese junks were traditional wooden sailing ships.

6 Fishing trawlers catch fish at sea.

1 lifeboat
2 ferry
3 Chinese junk
4 icebreaker
5 cargo ship
6 fishing trawler
7 aircraft carrier

Setting sail!

1 Clipper ships were fast sailing ships used in the 19th century.

Speedboats skim across water at high speed.

These are some of the most exciting ways to get from one place to another across water. **Which would you choose?**

3 People had to stand up to ride the first jet skis – sitting down is much safer!

5 Sailing yachts are medium-size boats with sails that can be used for racing or cruising.

4 The world's most expensive superyacht cost £3.85 billion.

The largest cruise ship in the world can hold more than 7,000 passengers.

1 clipper ship
2 speedboat
3 jet ski
4 superyacht
5 sailing yacht
6 cruise ship

Row, row, row your boat!

1. A coracle is a circular boat that is rowed with a paddle.

2. A raft is a flat, floating platform that can be steered with a paddle.

3. Kayaks were originally built by Inuit peoples.

4. Canoes are light, narrow boats with pointed ends.

5. Paddleboards are a type of surfboard you can stand up on.

Do you know the difference between an oar and a paddle? Oars are attached to the boat they are being rowed with, but paddles are loose and held in two hands. **Which of these would you like to set sail in?**

6 Rowing boats that are raced for sport are called "shells" (when someone rows with one oar) or "sculls" (when someone rows with two oars).

7 Rowing boats are often found on lakes in parks.

8 Dragon boats are traditionally Chinese and used for racing.

1 coracle	**3** kayak	**5** paddleboard	**7** rowing boat
2 raft	**4** canoe	**6** shell and scull	**8** dragon boat

Inland waterways

1 The Thames clipper is a fast riverboat that travels through the city of London.

3 Horse-drawn barges are traditionally painted with roses and flowers.

5 Gondolas have been used for more than 900 years.

Sometimes, the best way to see a place is from the water. Whether you live, work or are visiting somewhere new, boats travel through inland rivers and waterways all around the world.

2 Canal boats are often used for leisure, but they once were used for transporting goods around a country.

4 Glass-bottom boats let people see fish and sea life swimming below them.

6 Travellers on board river cruisers in places like Lake Kariba in Africa can look at the landscape and wildlife from observation decks.

- **1** riverboat
- **2** canal boat
- **3** horse-drawn barge
- **4** glass-bottom boat
- **5** gondola
- **6** river cruiser

Air and water power

1. When it starts moving fast, a hydrofoil lifts out of the water.
2. A curved board with a sail is used for windsurfing.
3. Surfing became an Olympic sport for the first time in 2020.

Engineers are working on producing wind-powered cars to give people a more environmentally friendly way to drive around. But these water-based vehicles already use wind, air or water for energy.

4 A catamaran has two separate hulls. The hull is the main part of the boat that sits in the water.

5 A sailing boat uses the wind caught in its sails to make it move.

6 Water hoverboards have water jets attached to the bottom that propel the board – and rider! – into the air.

1 hydrofoil

2 windsurf board

3 surfboard

4 catamaran

5 sailing boat

6 water hoverboard

Super submersibles

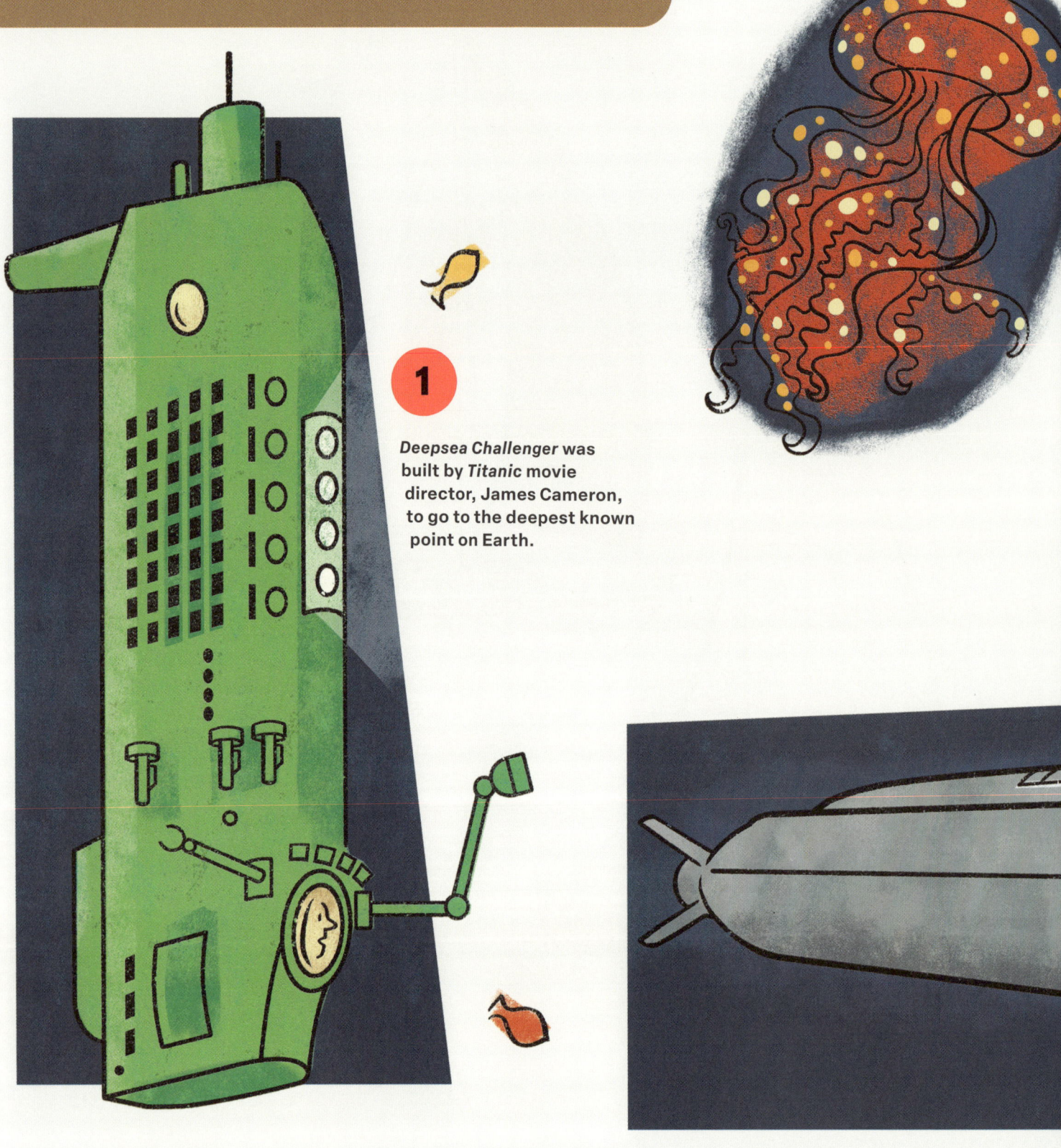

1

Deepsea Challenger was built by *Titanic* movie director, James Cameron, to go to the deepest known point on Earth.

An HOV is a Human-Operated Vehicle used for underwater scientific research. It's a submersible, which is a vehicle that is built to work while completely underwater. Not many people will get to go in one of these, but they are still pretty cool to know about!

2 *Alvin* is a submersible that can fit a pilot and two researchers to study the ocean floor.

3 Submarines can stay below the ocean's surface for up to four months at a time.

1 **Deepsea Challenger**   **2** *Alvin*   **3** submarine

In the air!

1 Hot air rises, so hot air balloons capture that air and use it to travel up in the sky.

2 There are all kinds of microlight and ultralight aircraft – some of them are very open, like this one.

Did you know that a flying car has been invented, but it isn't available to take for a ride yet? Let's go up, up and away!

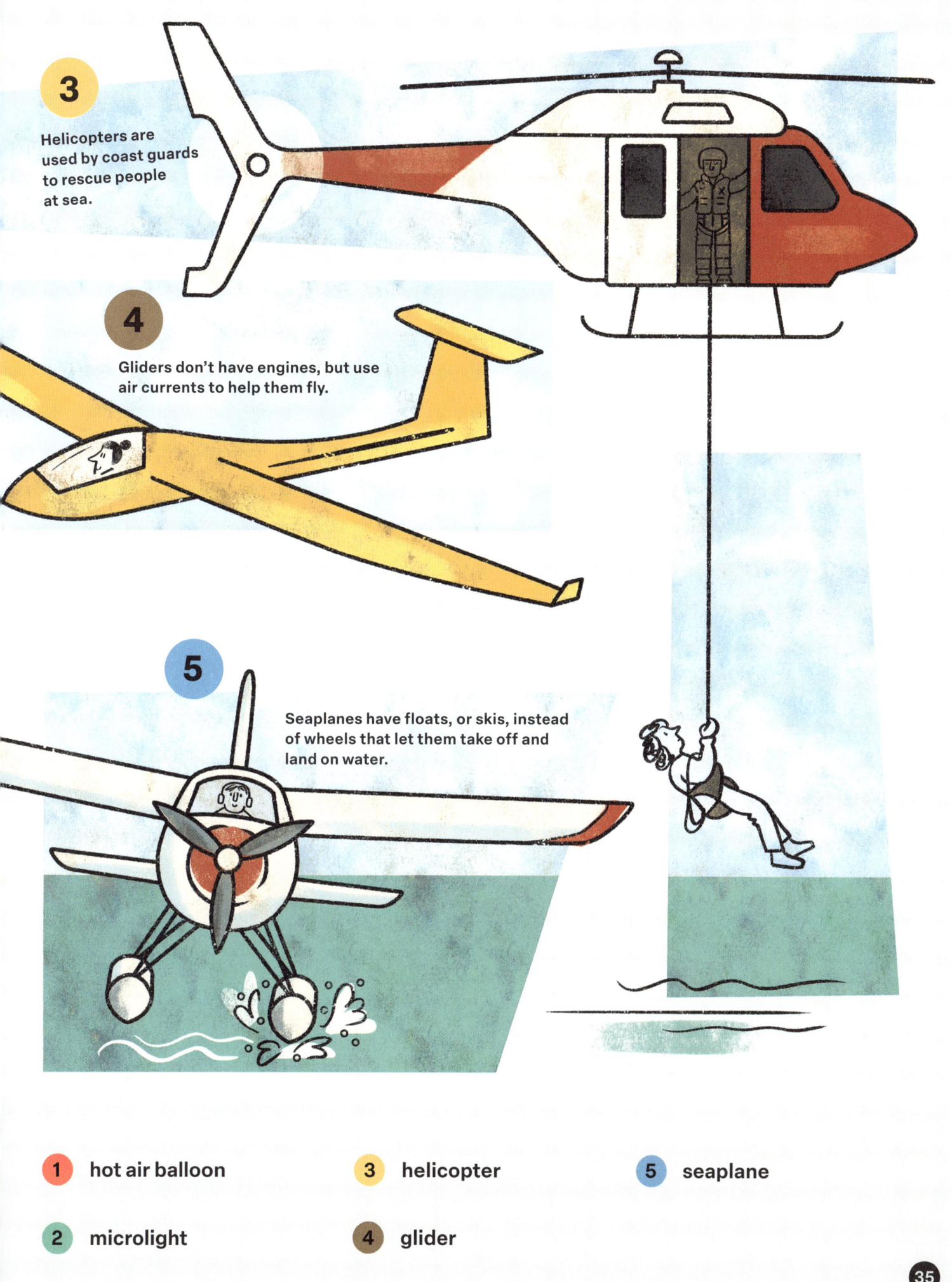

Wheels up!

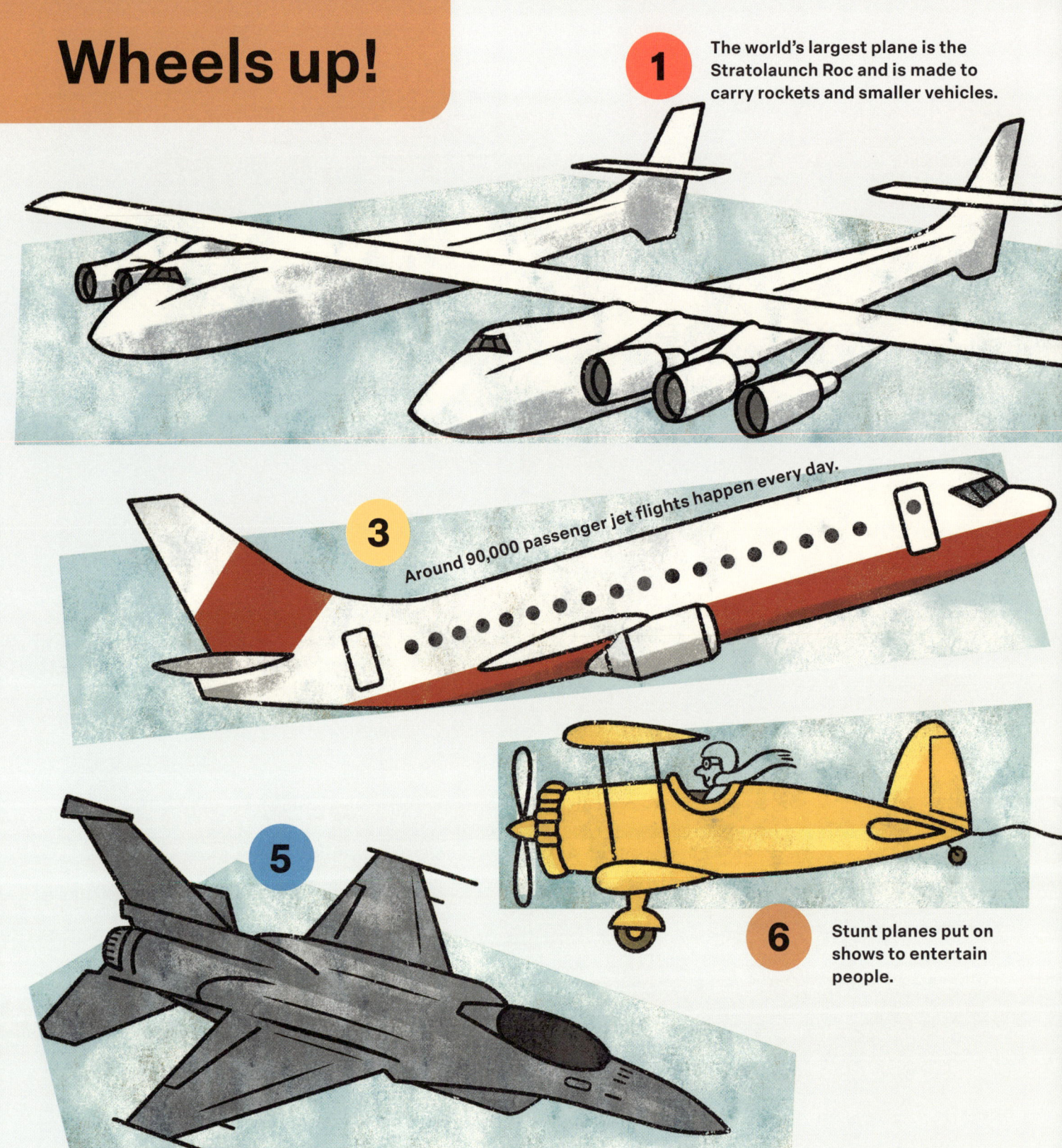

1 The world's largest plane is the Stratolaunch Roc and is made to carry rockets and smaller vehicles.

3 Around 90,000 passenger jet flights happen every day.

6 Stunt planes put on shows to entertain people.

Modern fighter planes travel at over 1,000 miles per hour (1,600kph)!

Did you know it takes around two years and 1,500 flying hours to qualify to become an airline pilot? Or that the president of the United States has a plane called Air Force One? Let's take off in one of these.

2 Crop dusters spray crops to protect them from insects and help them grow.

4 Stealth aircraft are invisible to radar.

SPRING STREET

7 Cargo aircraft transport goods instead of people.

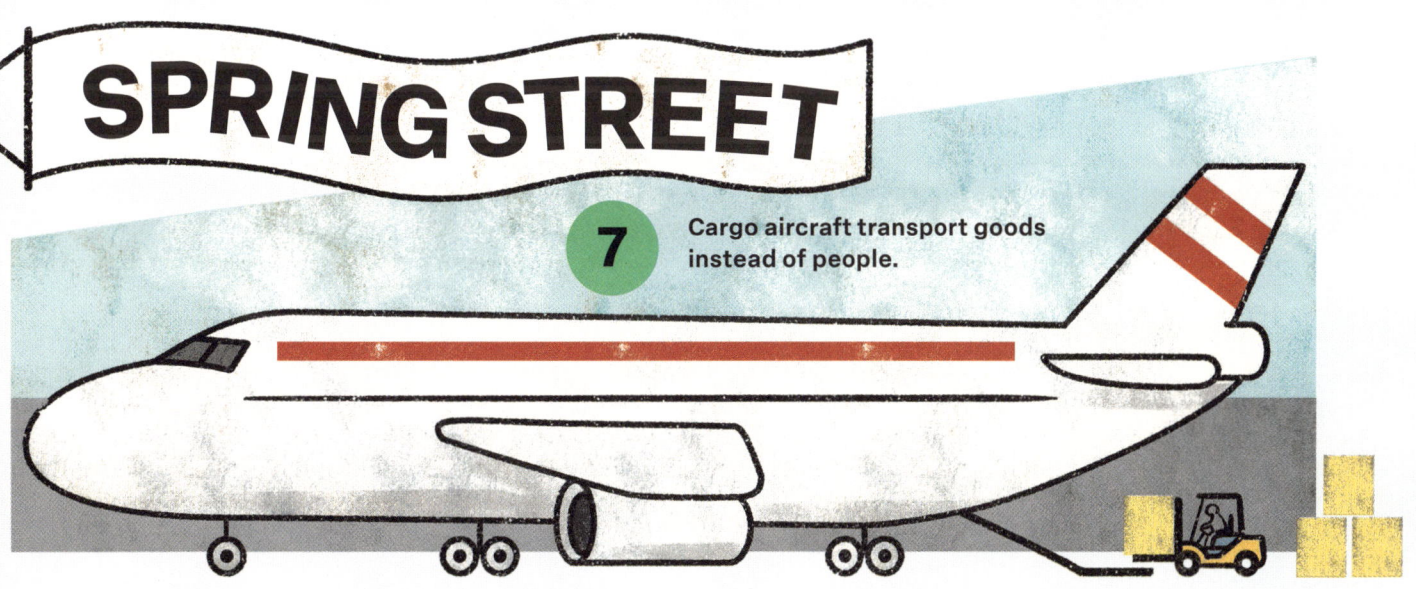

- **1** Stratolaunch Roc
- **2** crop duster
- **3** passenger jet
- **4** stealth aircraft
- **5** fighter aircraft
- **6** stunt plane
- **7** cargo plane

Rail power

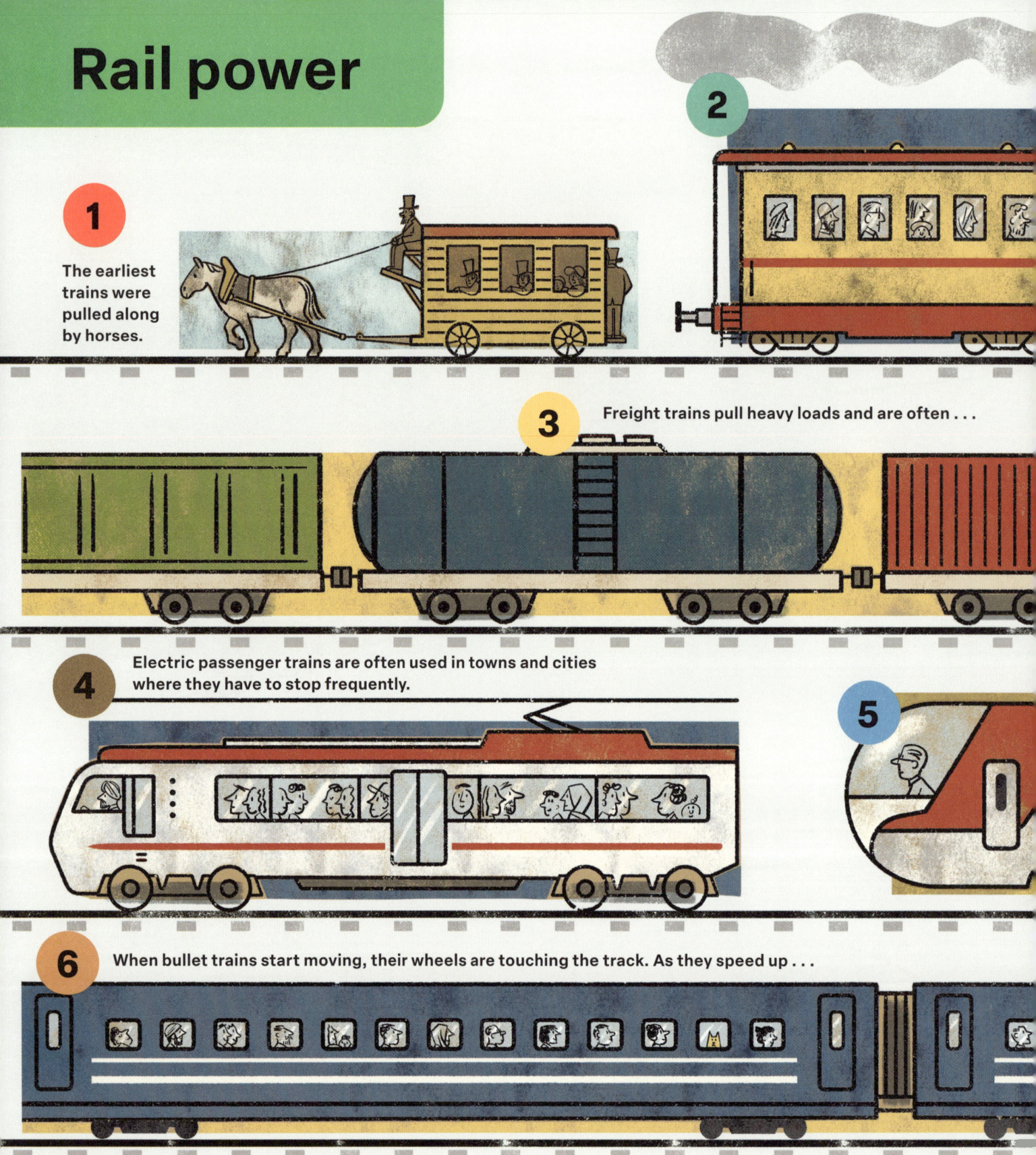

1 The earliest trains were pulled along by horses.

2

3 Freight trains pull heavy loads and are often . . .

4 Electric passenger trains are often used in towns and cities where they have to stop frequently.

5

6 When bullet trains start moving, their wheels are touching the track. As they speed up . . .

When trains were first invented, they relied on horses to pull them along. Then steam engines burned coal to power them. Today, most passenger trains are electric, but Japanese bullet trains are powered by magnetic levitation, which helps them reach speeds of up to 200 miles per hour (320kph).

Steam trains had a stoker who would shovel coal into the fire to keep the engine running.

. . . still powered by a fossil fuel called diesel.

There are no double-decker trains in the United Kingdom because so many bridges are too low.

. . . the wheels lift and the trains hover four inches (10cm) above the magnetic track.

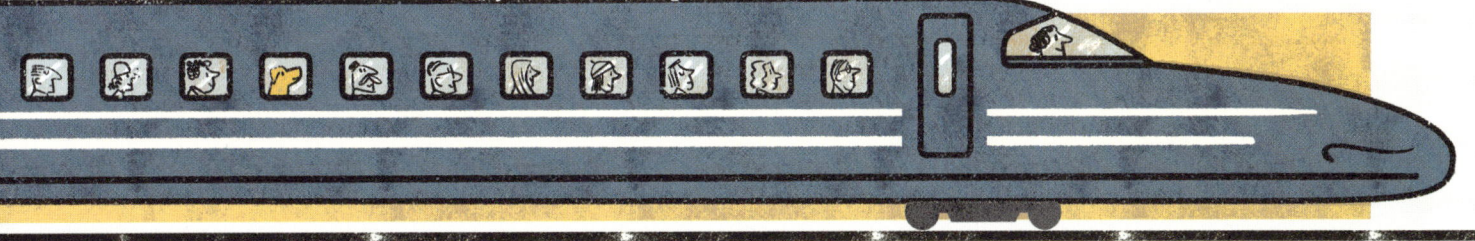

1. horse-powered train
2. steam train
3. freight train
4. electric passenger train
5. double-decker train
6. bullet train

Long and short rail journeys

1 Monorails have a single track – often above roads – to transport people in and out of urban areas.

2 Sleeper trains have beds for long overnight journeys.

Some railway trips can take a long time, and some are very short. However you're travelling, there's a form of rail travel for almost every distance.

3. Underground trains travel through tunnels beneath our feet.

4. APMs are Automated People Movers – you might see these in an airport or theme park to transport people around a small but busy space.

1. monorail 2. sleeper train 3. underground train 4. automated people mover

Connected to cables

1 San Francisco is a city that is famous for its cable tram.

2 Ski lifts take skiers up snowy mountains.

3 Funicular railways give people a way to get up very steep slopes.

Streetcars (also called trolleys or trams), unlike trains, usually run along public streets. Overhead cables also help to guide cars up steep hills and mountains. **Have you ever been in one of these?**

4 Visitors to tall landmarks such as Sugarloaf Mountain in Rio de Janeiro get fantastic views from cable cars (called aerial tramways in some parts of the world).

5 Streetcars are electric and transport people around busy cities.

1 cable tram

2 ski lift

3 funicular railway

4 cable car

5 streetcar

43

Lift off!

1 The Mars rover travels around the surface of Mars collecting samples and data.

2 Rockets are vehicles that launch into space.

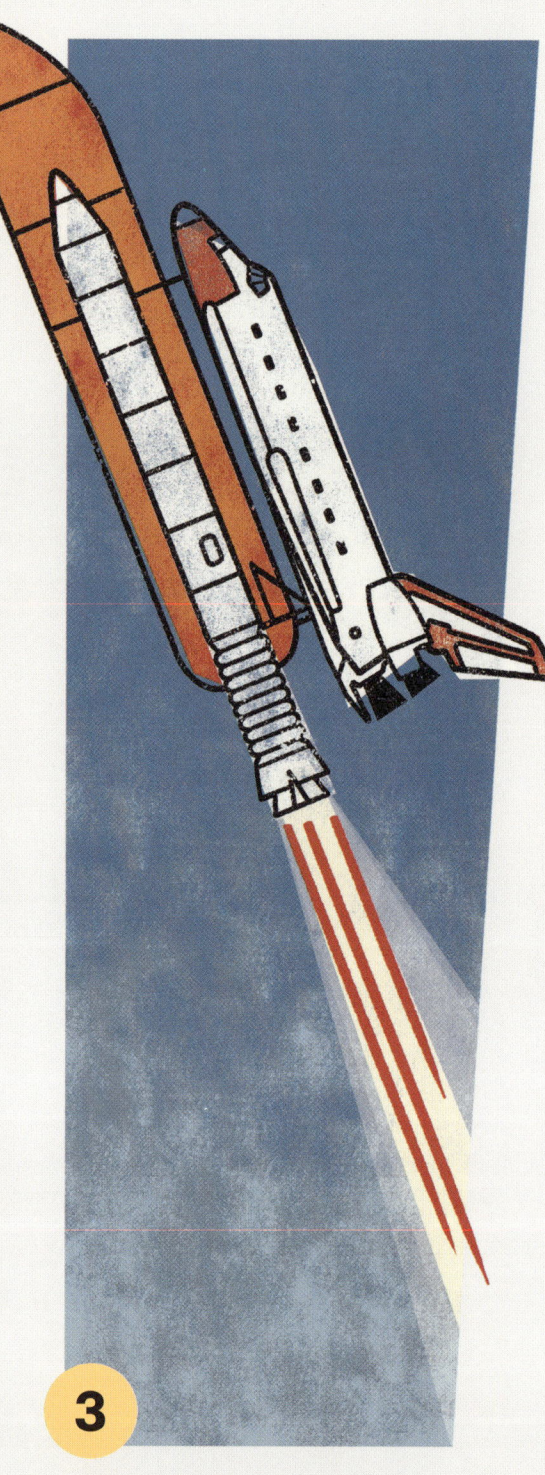

3 Space shuttles were vehicles that launched like rockets but landed like glider planes.

There are three NASA space shuttles in museums where people can visit them. NASA stands for National Aeronautics and Space Administration, an agency in the US that sends astronauts into space. The rest of these space vehicles are still being used to help us learn about our amazing universe.

4 The International Space Station (ISS) is a laboratory in space where astronauts live and work.

5 The Russian Soyuz spacecraft takes people and supplies to the ISS.

6 *Juno* is a spacecraft orbiting Jupiter to find out more about planet Earth.

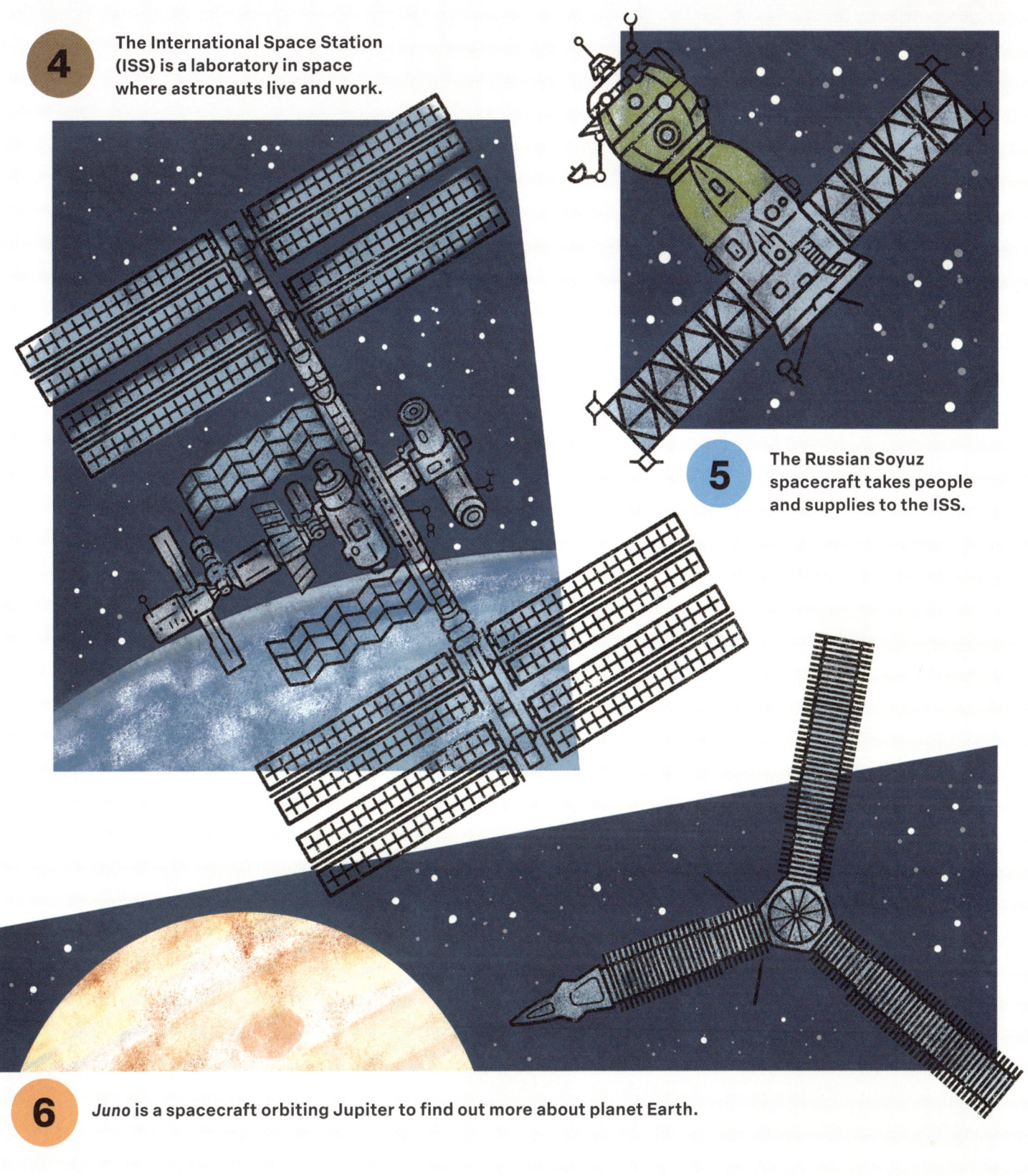

1. Mars rover
2. rocket
3. space shuttle
4. International Space Station
5. Soyuz
6. *Juno*